DON'T CRASH

AGAIN

A Car Accident
Victim's Guide
to Maximizing
Recovery

Printed in the United States of America
ISBN: 978-1-59571-859-4
Word Association Publishers
205 Fifth Avenue
Tarentum, Pennsylvania 15084
www.wordassociation.com

DON'T CRASH
AGAIN

A Car Accident
Victim's Guide
to Maximizing
Recovery

MICHAEL L. SAILE, JR., ESQ.

Contents

Introduction

Congratulations! You have made a wise decision to arm yourself with this important information before you begin to pursue your car accident injury case. By ordering this book, you have taken an active approach in your journey to recover fair compensation for that which a negligent driver took from you. This book will tell you what you should know before hiring a car accident lawyer.

This book was written to help level the playing field between big and powerful insurance companies and innocent accident victims. Experience demonstrates that auto insurance companies will do whatever it takes to minimize or eliminate your personal injury claim. An insurance company's business goal is to remain profitable by paying as little as possible on your claim. If you are not prepared to battle the insurance company, you will stand little chance of succeeding.

With every year that passes, insurance companies make it harder for accident victims to recover fair and reasonable compensation for their injuries. At the moment of impact, you entered a battlefield, and you will have a difficult fight ahead. Insurance companies have spent the last 30 years and hundreds of millions (possibly billions) of advertising dollars to negatively influence public opinion. The resulting deception is that the general public believes that all accident victims and personal injury trial lawyers are greedy, untruthful people.

Many people believe the TV commercials that portray insurance companies as friendly businesses. Insurance companies rely on this image but don't always live up to their promises. Insurance company representatives act like your best friend when you purchase insurance from them and when you pay your premiums. This all changes when you decide to make a claim against an auto insurance company for injuries, pain, and suffering. Suddenly, it's no more "Mr. Nice Guy"!

Unfortunately, insurance companies do an excellent job of convincing the general public that accident victims should not be awarded fair compensation for their pain and suffering. Juries across the country continuously award innocent accident victims little or no money for their pain and suffering.

By contrast, we believe that if you are genuinely injured by the carelessness or recklessness of another person, you should be fairly compensated. By reading this book, you will learn how to avoid some fatal mistakes when pursuing your claim. In addition, we will arm you with important insight and instruction so that you have a fighting chance to recover.

This book is divided into 11 sections that answer common questions involving car accident cases.

1. Should I speak with the other driver's insurance company?
2. Do I have a case?
3. How do I get my car fixed?
4. Who will pay my medical bills?
5. What if I miss time from work?
6. What kind of restrictions do I have on my insurance policy?
7. What types of doctors should I see?
8. Do I need a lawyer? How do I find one?
9. When will my case settle?
10. What does a lawsuit involve?
11. What should I do now?

Before you begin reading, you need to be aware that the information contained in this book is *not* legal advice. A lawyer-client relationship does not begin until an agreement has been signed by you and an attorney. This book will provide you with general information so that you can protect yourself and your claim before you hire a lawyer and, hopefully, before an insurance company takes advantage of you.

This book is *not* a substitute for a qualified personal injury trial lawyer's advice or services. We highly recommend that you pursue the services of a competent local car accident attorney for your case.

Section One:
Should I Speak with the Other Driver's Insurance Company

After a car accident, you have a duty to report the accident to your auto insurance company. Your auto insurance contract requires that you report the accident to your insurance company within a reasonable amount of time. If you do not report the accident to your auto insurance company, you may lose your insurance coverage. Don't make this mistake; when in doubt, report the accident. Most insurance companies have 24- hour claims service.

 INSIDER TIP
Report the car accident to your auto insurance company the same day as the accident.

Soon after the accident, you may get a telephone call or a letter from the other driver's insurance company. The other insurance company will attempt to take your statement over the phone. You should not give a statement to any auto insurance company other than your own. You have no legal duty to give them a statement. Don't even answer the phone if you know it's the other driver's insurance company calling! If you do answer, politely tell them that you are retaining a lawyer and your lawyer will be in contact with them soon.

Much like a criminal matter, any statement that you give to the other driver's auto insurance company may be used against you. If you have already made a statement or have spoken to the other driver or his or her insurance company, keep notes on exactly what you said, and inform your attorney about the statement or conversation.

 INSIDER TIP
Never give the other driver's insurance company a statement without a lawyer's advice

In addition to taking your statement, the other driver's insurance company may make you an offer to settle the case (just days after the accident). Do not accept this offer under any circumstances.

Insurance companies use these initial offers to take advantage of naïve car accident victims. These initial offers are rarely fair compensation. Neither you nor the other driver's insurance company can necessarily know the full extent of your pain or disabilities just days after the accident. Most often, these offers will also be available once you do know the severity and permanency of your injuries.

Section Two:
Do I Have a Case?

A personal injury case is a general name for several types of cases involving injuries caused by someone else's carelessness or recklessness. Vehicle accidents of all types including car, truck, or motorcycle accidents, slip and fall accidents, ATV or boating accidents, public transit accidents, work-related accidents, construction accidents, dangerous product injuries, and many others are commonly called "personal injury cases."

Although each case is different, most personal injury cases typically follow a similar course of events. First, there is the accident and injury, followed by medical treatment. Be aware: the medical treatment phase ends when you are discharged from medical care, not when you are released from an emergency care facility.

Once treatment has ended, you may try to settle your case with the insurance company. If you do not receive a fair and reasonable offer, you should think about filing a lawsuit.

So how do you know if you have a case? Three questions a lawyer will usually ask when evaluating a car accident case are:

1. Who is at fault?

2. What are your injuries?

3. Do you have a restriction in your auto insurance policy on your right to recover (sometimes known as limited tort or verbal threshold insurance)?

To determine who is at fault, lawyers and insurance companies use common sense and the rules of the road. You may be able to figure this out yourself. Police officers also must determine who was at fault before issuing a traffic violation for the accident. As a last resort, you will go to court where a judge asks a jury, comprised of ordinary people without any formal legal training, to determine who was at fault.

Simply put, if the accident was your fault, you probably don't have a case for pain and suffering. If you are injured and someone else is at fault, then you should continue to read this book.

Once fault is determined and it appears that you are not at fault or are less at fault than the other party involved, a lawyer will want to know what injuries you have sustained. This analysis includes an evaluation of the extent and permanency of your injuries or disabilities, and how the accident affects and will continue to affect your life.

The third inquiry is whether you have a restriction of your right to recovery for your pain and suffering by having selected a "limited tort" (sometimes termed verbal threshold) auto insurance policy. Tort selection will be explained in Section Six of this book.

In a car accident lawsuit, the injured person is known as the plaintiff. The defendant is the person, business, or government entity that has directly or indirectly caused your injuries. Sometimes there may be more than one defendant in a case.

Your matter is known as a "claim" until you or your lawyer files a lawsuit against the defendant. You begin a lawsuit by filing a legal document called a "complaint" with the clerk of court in the county where the accident occurred. The complaint tells the court and the defendant that you want the civil justice system to determine how you should be compensated for your medical bills, lost wages, injuries, and pain and suffering. The words "case" and "claim" are often interchangeable.

Under many state laws, including Pennsylvania and New Jersey, you must file a car accident injury complaint (begin a lawsuit) with the court on or before the second anniversary of your car accident. There are some limited circumstances where this rule does not apply. Most lawyers will not file a lawsuit immediately after an accident because at that time, the extent and permanency of your injuries is still unknown. In some cases, the full extent and severity of your injuries cannot be determined until many months have passed.

 INSIDER TIP
In many states, including PA & NJ, a car accident lawsuit must be filed with the court within two years of the date of the accident. Check the rule in your state.

If someone else has caused your injuries and you have measurable physical and/or mental injuries, you may have a case worth pursuing. Further analysis can determine the value of your case. Only a lawyer with local car accident case experience should help you make this determination. Don't let the insurance company do it for you!

Section Three:
How Do I Get My Car Fixed?

When a claim is made against an insurance company for damage to a vehicle, this claim is known as a property damage claim. The task of finding a repair shop to fix your vehicle or replacing the vehicle if it was totaled is usually conducted by its owner, often you or a family member. Because vehicle values are more easily determined than injury values, and sometimes the legal fees exceed the cost of the auto repairs, lawyers do not typically get involved with the property damage claim.

When your car is damaged by another person's negligence, you may have the option to choose who will repair your vehicle. First, you must analyze the insurance coverage for the accident. You can easily determine whether you have collision coverage (otherwise known as property damage coverage) on your auto insurance policy by checking the declarations page of your policy. If you do not understand the declarations page, you can simply call your auto insurance company for an explanation.

INSIDER TIP
Locate the DECLARATIONS PAGE of your auto insurance policy to determine your collision coverage.

Most drivers carry collision coverage on their vehicles. This is because most finance companies require it to protect the vehicle (the collateral on their car loan). Sometimes it may not make sense to carry collision coverage on a vehicle, especially when the vehicle is older and does not justify the cost of the collision coverage.

You should also determine whether the other driver was insured. In many states, the other driver's insurance company is listed on the police accident report. You can then obtain the insurance company's contact information online.

 I N S I D E R   T I P
As soon as possible, order a copy of the accident report from the local or state police department that responded to the accident.

At this point you, or preferably your attorney, should report the car accident to the other driver's insurance company. It is important that you do not give a full statement to the other driver's insurance company. You may have to briefly explain where, when, and how the accident occurred. Be extremely brief when you report the accident to the other driver's insurance company. Do not discuss your injuries, medical treatment, employment, or any other aspect of your personal situation. The other driver's insurance company should then inform you whether or not the other driver was insured.

INSIDER TIP
When setting up a claim with the other driver's insurance company for damage to your vehicle, do not discuss anything, except how the crash occurred and the condition of your vehicle.

If you have collision coverage of your own and the other driver was insured, you then have the option to use either auto insurance company to repair your car. If you decide to use your insurance company, you may receive faster and friendlier service. There may be some limitations. When you purchased your auto insurance, you may or may not have selected car rental coverage. If you did not, you may be stranded for a few days. Your insurance company may also dictate what repair shops to use and whether new or used replacement vehicle parts will be used to repair your car.

If you choose to utilize your insurance policy to repair your vehicle, your insurance company will seek payment from the other driver's insurance company. Before your insurance company recovers payment from the other driver's insurance company, you will have to pay the deductible associated with your property damage coverage to the vehicle repair facility.

On the other hand, the other driver who caused the accident has a duty under the law to "make you whole." This would include a rental vehicle comparable to your damaged vehicle and the opportunity to use a body shop of your choice. The other driver's insurance company may not handle your property damage claim as quickly as you expect. In some circumstances, your auto insurance company may also be the other driver's insurance company. In that case, the choice of auto insurance companies does not matter.

If the insurance company believes that your car is totaled (not worth fixing), then you need to determine the current value of your vehicle. This can be done online by one of the many free vehicle valuation websites. We suggest that you appraise your vehicle on several different websites.

 INSIDER TIP

Don't trust the insurance company to give you a fair value for your totaled vehicle. Conduct your own independent research and be prepared to negotiate a fair amount.

The insurance company will also determine the value of your vehicle. Insurance companies have a more complicated method of valuing your vehicle, which includes consideration of local auction prices and local used car sale prices. You can then compare your appraised value with the insurance company's value to determine whether you are receiving a fair value for your vehicle.

You may need to negotiate with the insurance company to raise their initial offer to fair value. You can use your vehicle appraisals to help you negotiate. Usually, a property damage settlement is reached at a value between the insurance company's initial offer and your appraised value.

To begin the process, you should promptly obtain a copy of the police accident report and determine whether you have collision coverage on the declarations page of your insurance policy. If you have no coverage on your policy, you will have no choice but to use the other driver's insurance company. Use caution. If you run into trouble with the other driver's auto insurance company, you should have an experienced car accident lawyer handle the property damage claim for you.

Section Four:
Who Will Pay My Medical Bills?

All drivers are required by law to have a certain minimum coverage of auto insurance coverage for their own medical bills, though the amount varies by state. We usually recommend that you purchase more than the minimum coverage.

You may be surprised to learn that in many states, you (through your insurance company) are partially responsible for paying your own medical bills. Many states have what is called "no fault" auto insurance. This means that no matter who was at fault for the accident, each party pays for his or her own medical bills up to the amount of the insurance coverage.

INSIDER TIP
For future protection, call your auto insurance agent and increase the limits of your auto insurance coverage for medical expenses.

What happens once you have used up the medical coverage portion of your auto insurance? After your auto insurance is exhausted, your health insurance company may then be responsible to pay your medical bills. If you don't have health insurance, it is extremely important to have adequate automobile insurance.

If you don't have adequate auto and health insurance, you may not be able to obtain the proper medical treatment required for your health and for your car accident case. Some car accident victims rely on a government assistance program such as Medicaid if they do not have health insurance.

A problem arises if you use Medicaid or certain health insurance plans to pay for your accident-related medical bills. The problem it creates is called a lien. A lien is a legal right to a portion of your settlement or jury award. Medicaid and some health insurance plans have the legal right to be reimbursed the amount paid for your medical bills. Believe it or not, even though you paid health insurance premiums each month, some private plans also have the right to be reimbursed from your recovery.

When you obtain health insurance, you should determine whether the health insurance company has a right to be repaid for the medical bills that it pays for your treatment as a result of an accident. Unfortunately, most people do not have health insurance options since they obtain health insurance from their employers. If this is true in your case, you will simply have whatever your employer offers, but it is helpful to know which one you have so that you can purchase more medical coverage on your auto insurance policy.

INSIDER TIP
Request a copy of your health insurance policy so that you can determine whether there may be a lien on your case recovery.

If you can afford it, you always have the right to pay for your own medical treatment. If you pay for your own medical treatment, your out-of-pocket medical bills will be part of your claim against the other party. Likewise, if there is a lien on your settlement for medical bills, the lien amount can be added to your claim against the other party.

If you have a good relationship with your doctor, he or she may treat you knowing that you may have a future car accident case recovery. In this situation, your doctor will request a "letter of protection" from your attorney. This letter means that the doctor will treat you now, but you must pay the doctor back from the proceeds of your settlement or jury verdict.

Section Five:
What If I Miss Time from Work?

Many car accident victims are faced with the decision of whether to go back to work or stay home to recuperate. The emergency room doctors should give you some insight as to when you should return to work. If not, we highly recommend that you do not return to work until you have followed up with your family doctor.

Your family doctor is usually in the best position to determine whether you should be resting or are healthy enough to go back to work. If you are not permitted to return to work, your family doctor can write a note excusing you from work.

 I N S I D E R   T I P
Call your family doctor and insist that
he or she examine you within two days
after the car accident.

Are you a fighter? A fighter is a person who will use his or her best efforts to fight through pain and not be disabled by injuries. Often he or she will fight through the pain associated with performing employment duties.

Working while you should be resting could make your medical condition worse and may be harmful to your car accident case. In a car accident case, an insurance company or jury members may not understand that you are a fighter, which can really be detrimental to your case–because they may take the position that you are not as badly injured as you claim to be. When in doubt, take a few days off to allow your body to recover.

Your auto insurance policy may have wage loss coverage available for missed work. Proper wage loss documentation must be submitted to your insurance company in order to receive wage loss benefits, including a doctor's note, proof from your employer that you missed work, and proof of the amount of your wages or salary.

 INSIDER TIP

If your family depends on your weekly paycheck, make sure that you have lost wage coverage on your auto insurance policy.

You also have the right to recover lost wages from the person who caused the car accident. In most cases, the other party's insurance company will not reimburse you for lost wages until a full settlement or a jury verdict is reached on the entire claim. For many families, this creates a major financial burden because a settlement may not happen for months or even years after the accident.

If you are permanently injured from a car accident and can no longer work, you may be eligible to receive federal Social Security disability benefits. To receive these benefits, you must be disabled by a medical condition that is expected to last at least one year. You should consult with an experienced attorney before applying for this type of assistance.

When a car accident victim who was employed is seriously injured, lost wages (including future lost wages) often make up the majority of the value of the claim. With the help of vocational and economic experts, an attorney can project the amount of lost wages that an individual would have earned throughout his or her career and argue for that amount.

Section Six:
What Kind of Restrictions Do I Have on My Insurance Policy?

"Tort" is a legal word for an injury, damage, or wrong caused either intentionally or negligently to another. A car accident is one example of a tort. The type of tort coverage you purchase on your policy determines what restrictions limit the amount you are able to recover in the event of a car accident.

Under most states' laws, all registered automobiles must be insured. In some states, including Pennsylvania and New Jersey, lawmakers have decided that it would be beneficial to give drivers an option known as a "tort option" to help reduce the costs of mandatory auto insurance. As a result, when a driver purchases auto insurance, he or she has two choices—full tort or limited tort (sometimes called verbal threshold) insurance.

Many drivers make the uneducated decision of opting out of full tort insurance because limited tort (or verbal threshold) insurance is less expensive. Although full tort insurance is more costly, we highly recommend that you keep full tort auto insurance. It is important because the tort option that you choose not only binds you, but also binds all household relatives, including your children.

Full tort coverage means that a person who is injured in a car accident caused by someone else can sue the negligent person for pain and suffering damages without any restrictions.

INSIDER TIP
Select a full tort auto insurance policy.
Do not compromise!

Each state has its own exceptions to the limited tort or verbal threshold law and it is always advisable to have an attorney examine your situation. In most states, including Pennsylvania and New Jersey, if you have suffered a serious injury you may be able to get past your limited tort or verbal threshold restriction and recover for your pain and suffering. Generally, there must be medical evidence, including physician testimony and positive objective medical testing, to pass the limited tort or verbal threshold test for a "serious type of injury."

In many such cases, the insurance company's lawyer will petition the court to dismiss your case for failure to pass the specific requirement. Only an experienced car accident lawyer will know if you meet any of the limited tort exceptions and will be fully prepared to present your particular case in court.

INSIDER TIP
Don't be fooled! "Full coverage" does
not mean "full tort." Full coverage is a
general name for when your car is protected by property damage coverage.

Choosing limited or verbal threshold tort has its consequences. Many car accident victims suffer severe pain and take medication everyday but cannot recover any money because their medical testing did not show a serious type of injury. Don't make this mistake – choose full tort auto insurance!

Section Seven:
What Types of Doctors Should I See?

When you are discharged from the hospital, you will be released to deal with your pain. Typically, the first evening after the accident is when the pain really begins to set in. The most important thing to do at this point is to follow the instructions given to you at the hospital. In most cases, the emergency room doctors will have also given you prescriptions for pain-killers (narcotics) and muscle relaxers.

Prior to being discharged, one of the nurses should have reviewed "discharge instructions" with you and given you a written copy to take home. Discharge instructions provide you with a description of your injury, the medications that you should take, and instructions on how to treat your injuries.

One common instruction is to follow up with your family doctor. When you return home, you should immediately call your family doctor to set up an appointment. It is important to be assertive with your doctor's office so that you obtain an appointment within two days.

At this appointment, you should ask your family doctor if he or she regularly treats car accident injury patients. Confirm that your family doctor is qualified and comfortable in treating complex neck and spine injuries. It is okay to question this, because many family doctors are not experienced or well versed in handling traumatic neck and spine injuries. If this is the case, ask for a referral from your family doctor for a qualified doctor who regularly treats car accident injuries.

Not only must your injuries be properly treated, but your doctor must be able to medically document your specific injuries so that they can be proven to a jury. Some doctors are very good at working with personal injury cases. However, other doctors shy away from this type of treatment. Stay away from these doctors, as they will only hurt you and your case.

Your doctor must be willing and able to write comprehensive medical reports. Many doctors do not want to spend the time to do this. Ultimately, if your case does not settle, your doctor must testify in court to help prove your injuries, pain, and disabilities. Some doctors refuse to testify. Other doctors charge an outrageous fee to go to court. Do not let yourself fall into this trap. There are plenty of qualified, skilled, and interested doctors who can meet your needs.

 INSIDER TIP

Don't be shy. Question your family doctor about his or her experience with treating accident victims. Find a doctor who regularly treats traumatic injuries.

It is also important that you are referred to the proper medical specialists. These doctors are trained to identify specific injuries and administer specific types of treatment. Common medical specialists for car accident injuries include: orthopedists, neurologists, radiologists, surgeons, pain management doctors, and chiropractors.

Your lawyer should not refer you directly to a doctor. A personal injury lawyer can make you aware of certain doctors in a specialty, but should not make the final decision for you. Consider this: attorneys for insurance companies have been known to trick juries. When a jury hears that your lawyer sent you to a specific doctor, the jurors are led to believe that your case is fake—that you, the doctor, and your attorney have manufactured your case. Don't let your lawyer make this fatal mistake. You, your family doctor, and your loved ones should make your medical decisions.

It is also important that you keep a daily journal. Each day your journal should record:

1. The location, intensity, and duration of your pain.

2. Any physical and mental restrictions that you experienced due to your injuries and pain.

3. Any medications taken, including both prescribed and over-the-counter.

4. Any doctor appointments that you attended and the type of treatment that you received.

5. Any activities, hobbies, or employment duties that you could not perform because of your pain and restrictions.

6. Any activities, hobbies, or employment duties that you did perform or partially performed, but with pain and restrictions.

A daily journal will give your lawyer, an insurance company, a judge, and a jury the best insight into how you have suffered day by day. This is your chance to effectively communicate how the accident has affected you. You should keep your journal every day until your case has ended.

INSIDER TIP
Many people begin to keep a daily journal but then quit after a few weeks. If you quit keeping your daily journal, insurance companies and juries may believe that you have recovered.

The most important thing to do during your medical treatment is to follow your doctor's instructions. Whether you are being treated by your family doctor, a chiropractor, an orthopedist, a neurologist, or a pain management doctor, each physician will have a care plan for you to follow. This care plan may include medication, diet restrictions, stretching, rest, sleep, physical therapy, exercises, and doctor appointments.

Do not miss any doctor appointments. If you miss medical appointments, you will damage your case. An auto insurance company will eventually review your claim, and review and analyze your doctor's visits. Any gaps in medical treatment may be used against you. Insurance companies routinely take the position that if you miss recommended medical treatment appointments, then you must feel better and do not require treatment. There may be many reasons why you are not be able to attend an appointment, but you should be aware that any significant break in treatment will hurt your personal injury case.

 INSIDER TIP
Do not miss doctor appointments.
If you miss medical treatmen
appointments of any kind, it
may be used against you.

At this point, it is time to think about whether you need to hire a lawyer. Before you contact a lawyer, you should gather together all of your car insurance documents. A lawyer will also need a list of the names and addresses of your medical providers and a copy of the police accident report. All of this information is critical to begin your injury claim.

Section Eight:
Do I Need a Lawyer? How Do I Find One?

After reading this book, you may think that you need to hire a lawyer, but in some cases this may not be true. In certain cases, where the other party is clearly at fault and has minimal auto insurance, the other party's insurance company may offer you the entire insurance policy limits. You should be careful before accepting an offer in this situation, because you always have the option to sue the other party responsible for the car accident to seek their personal assets. This decision will depend upon the severity of your injuries, the total amount of insurance coverage, and the assets of the party who caused the accident. If you are not knowledgeable in these areas, you may make a big mistake by immediately settling your claim.

Generally, people who have little insurance coverage have minimal assets. People who have substantial assets usually protect those assets with more insurance coverage. An experienced lawyer should help you properly evaluate this situation.

In other instances, a lawyer may not accept your case. Generally, this happens when the case is so small that the amount recovered will not be worth the time that a lawyer must devote to your case. Claims for only damage to your vehicle typically fall into this category. Some lawyers will not accept limited tort (verbal threshold) cases.

INSIDER TIP

If you are in doubt about whether to hire a lawyer, take the time to have a free consultation with a local personal injury lawyer.

We highly recommend that you obtain a lawyer if you are badly injured. This book does not discuss trial theory or strategy because if your case gets as far as filing a lawsuit, you should have a lawyer. In all likelihood, without a lawyer, complicated evidence and court rules that require experience and legal knowledge will ground your case. Only an experienced car accident attorney can present your case effectively at trial.

If you are truly injured, you will find that your injuries, pain, and restrictions will consume your life. What can be more personal than getting the right treatment for your injuries and recovering a fair amount of money for your pain and suffering, lost wages, and other out-of-pocket expenses? Your family may be depending on your recovery. Your suffering and financial loss not only affects you, but also affects your spouse, your children, and others.

State legislators have created complex rules and laws that deal with every aspect of a personal injury case. These laws get more complicated every year. In addition to the written law, trial and appellate courts issue opinions that interpret the written laws.

Would you try to drill your own teeth to fix cavities or would you go to a dentist? You may have the tools such as a drill, a mirror, and some pain medication to do it yourself, but wouldn't you prefer someone who is educated, professionally trained, and experienced to work on such an important personal matter? The same should apply to your personal injury claim. At the very least, consult with a lawyer. Consultations are usually free.

How do you find the right lawyer?

You may think it's easy to find a good car accident lawyer. Many injury lawyers spend lots of money advertising in the Yellow Pages, in newspapers, on TV commercials, on billboards, on buses, and online. So how do you know which attorney will be the best to suit your needs?

Open the Yellow Pages and take a look at the 50+ pages of lawyer advertisements. They all say the same things: "Serious Injury Lawyer," "No recovery—No Fee," "Free Consultations"…etc. Besides different photos and graphics, don't they all look the same?

How do you determine which of these lawyers is right for you? The phone book is not a good place to find the right lawyer. The same goes for internet directories of lawyers. There are more effective ways to find a car accident lawyer.

Personal recommendations

Recommendations from people whom you trust are generally the most effective way to find a good lawyer for your case. Personal experience is the preferred way to gain insight about any professional, including a lawyer's service, knowledge, personality, and ability.

Close friends, family members, and trusted business contacts will provide you with the best recommendations. Although not guaranteed, past experience may be the best way to predict a future experience.

Be cautioned: another person's experience may not be the same as yours. The lawyer and the other person may have had a special personal relationship. They may have discovered that they have something in common, or for any number of reasons, the lawyer may have had more time to devote to the other person's case.

A lawyer who focuses on car accident law

This is an important consideration. A large percentage of lawyers, especially lawyers in small law firms, practice personal injury law. You need to determine whether these lawyers really know what they are doing.

It's easy for a lawyer to meet with you, but what happens when the insurance company denies your claim or offers you a pittance? Many lawyers who do not focus on car accident law will not have the knowledge, skills, and conviction necessary to fight an insurance company. Lawyers are busy people, and unless they focus on car accident law, they may miss the latest legal developments. A good car accident lawyer keeps up with the latest jury trends and effective trial techniques.

Courts constantly issue new case opinions that change the law. It is important that the lawyer you choose knows how local judges are likely to rule on the latest court opinions. If a judge is not aware of the latest rule of law, it is the lawyer's job to let the judge know about the new law to advocate on your behalf.

A lawyer who has litigation experience

You might be shocked to learn that many lawyers are afraid to go to court—just as afraid as you may be, or more so. This even includes those lawyers who have big advertisements in the Yellow Pages. Beware of lawyers who are afraid to go to trial (of course they may never admit it). You can find out by asking how many accident cases the lawyer has taken on, how many of them he or she has taken to trial, and how many were won. Some lawyers are afraid to go to court because it is intimidating. In addition to knowing the law and your case, with everyone's attention focused on him or her, your lawyer must be comfortable standing and speaking in front of a judge, a jury, and a room full of people.

Insurance companies usually know if your lawyer is afraid to go to court. They keep track of lawyers and their performance on past cases. They share this information with other insurance companies. Insurance companies don't just evaluate you and your injuries; they also evaluate your lawyer. Insurance companies may make a lesser offer on your case if they know that your lawyer is one who will want to settle instead of putting up a fight by taking your case to trial.

Some lawyers do not want to risk their time and money if they lose. What is the value of a car accident lawyer if he or she is not willing to take a worthy case to trial? If a car accident lawyer accepts your case, he or she should prepare your case from the very beginning as if it will go to trial.

A lawyer who has the time to devote to you and your case

Good lawyers are busy people. Unfortunately, it will be almost impossible for you to determine whether a lawyer will spend adequate time on your case. Therefore, during your initial consultation, you should ask:

1. How many cases he or she is currently handling

2. How complex these cases are

3. How much time he or she plans to devote to your case

4. What his or her case acceptance guidelines are.

Clients commonly complain about a lack of communication with their lawyers. Many of these clients believe their lawyers are not working on their cases. In some of those instances, the lawyer is working on the case but is not keeping the client informed. Generally, your lawyer should keep you informed as much as reasonably possible.

A client should be educated on the law by his or her attorney and should be involved in most decisions. A full understanding of the process not only lets the client know what is happening in the case, but also empowers the client with information. This type of interaction keeps a client interested and better prepares him or her to be a better witness, if and when he or she is called upon to testify in court. We have found that most injured victims want to be informed and learn about their cases.

We will let you in on a little secret that other lawyers will not like us to reveal…the less time a lawyer spends on a personal injury case, the more profitable the case is for the lawyer. Fast and easy settlements add up to big lawyer profits. If a lawyer settles a case early (spending little time and money on the case), he or she can do this for many cases at a time.

You should be wary of a lawyer with no case acceptance guidelines. Law firms that run this type of practice are referred to as personal injury "mills." Your case could be just one out of several hundred cases being juggled by the lawyer. Don't fall victim to this type of practice. A competent and ethical personal injury lawyer will only take on the cases to which he or she can devote the proper amount of time and resources.

A lawyer who is going to handle your case from beginning to end

Many firms have a recognizable senior attorney whose name is on the door. You have probably seen these firms advertised on TV. People think, "Wow! They are on TV… they must make a lot of money. If they make a lot of money they must be good." Don't fall into this trap.

Those "figure head" attorneys may not have stepped into a courtroom for years. They may meet with their clients (but not often) and hand them settlement checks once the cases have settled. Unbeknownst to the client, young associates, paralegals (who are not lawyers), and other staff do most of the work. Some of these lawyers even let their non-lawyer staff negotiate client settlements with the insurance companies.

Be aware that some lawyers will terminate their representation of a client if the case does not settle before the second anniversary of the car accident. These lawyers will refer the case to another attorney who will take the case to trial. They in turn collect a referral fee from the trial attorney. To maximize your chance of recovery, you should seek a lawyer who will handle your case from beginning to end rather than referring you to another attorney in the middle of your claim.

A lawyer who is compassionate

Our nation's Constitution has many protections. One of our protections is the right to a trial by a jury of peers. This is a personal right providing that if someone does a "harm" or a "wrong" to you, you can recover for that harm in a civil manner. It is your lawyer's responsibility to make your voice heard.

A personal injury trial lawyer must be a compassionate advocate for his or her clients and should have the drive to help innocent car accident victims recover fair compensation. During your first meeting, you should be able to determine if the lawyer has the conviction to fight for you.

A lawyer with a fair fee agreement

Every state has different ethical rules and customs that determine how car accident lawyers may charge their fees. One common type is a contingent fee agreement. Lawyers are permitted to use contingent fee agreements with car accident cases. Most injured clients prefer this type of agreement.

A contingent fee agreement is an arrangement where a lawyer gets paid for his or her time spent on the case only when and if there is a recovery of money from the case. A lawyer will sometimes provide for the expenses of a lawsuit, which could amount to tens of thousands of dollars in some cases. The recovery from the case is then divided between the client, the lawyer, and sometimes the medical providers.

In many states, there is no rule setting the exact percentage that a lawyer may charge a client for a car accident case. The only boundaries are ethical rules that require that the fee must be "fair and reasonable."

What is fair and reasonable? Frequently, lawyers charge a 40, 45, or even a 50 percent contingency fee in personal injury cases. This fee is charged before all case expenses are paid. Does that seem fair? Doesn't it make more sense that the less work a lawyer does, the less he or she should be paid?

Consider this: the standard contingent fee agreement used by most car accident lawyers works the opposite way. Some lawyers do not want to perform the extra work needed to obtain a higher settlement or verdict, so they recommend settling the case early. If a lawyer settles a case early, the lawyer gets a huge benefit. Avoid this type of situation. Seek a contingency fee agreement that rewards you, rather than the lawyer, if your case settles early. If a lawyer is not willing to have such an arrangement, perhaps you should find another lawyer.

Section Nine:
When Will My Case Settle?

A personal injury victim's primary focus should be his or her health. You will find that at the end of your case, whether you win or lose, you would rather not have been injured. At the end of the case, the judge, jury, lawyers, doctors, and the defendant will walk away from your accident case without any further thought. You, however, will live with your injuries for the rest of your life. No amount of money will be able to take away your permanent pain or repair your disabilities.

INSIDER TIP

Many car accident victims look for quick settlements. In most cases, quick settlements are not fair compensation. You must have patience. The majority of car accident cases do not settle within the first year.

After your doctors release you from treatment, you should notify your attorney so that he or she can request final medical reports. It may take several weeks for your doctor to issue a final report. You should also set up a meeting with your attorney to discuss the progress of your treatment and to create a plan for the next stage of your claim—the negotiation stage.

Once your attorney receives the final medical reports and medical bills, he or she should be ready to draft a demand letter. This letter is a complete chronological description of your experience from the date of the car accident to the present. A demand letter usually starts with a description of when, where, and how the accident happened, followed by your medical treatment, your current complaints of pain, wage loss, and other out-of-pocket expenses.

The demand letter will end with a demand for a certain amount of money. Copies of the police report, ambulance report, hospital records, medical records, photographs, witness statements, and other pertinent information are included with the demand package.

A demand letter is a critical step in your case and should be prepared by an experienced car accident lawyer. The demand letter should be drafted in a clear and convincing manner that presents your case in the best light. A demand letter is the insurance company's first look at your entire claim.

Some law firms give the task of drafting a demand letter to their secretaries or paralegals, who are not lawyers. These people do not have the legal training or expertise necessary to create persuasive arguments to convince the insurance company that you are entitled to be fully compensated for your injuries.

After the demand letter and all accompanying documents are sent to the insurance company, it usually takes a few weeks for an insurance company's adjuster to review the package. In some cases, the adjuster must review the case with a supervisor in order to obtain permission to make an offer. In larger cases, the insurance adjuster may have to meet with a panel of insurance company managers to get permission to make an offer. Once an adjuster obtains permission to offer money, he or she will contact you (or your lawyer, if you have retained one) to discuss and negotiate the case.

So how do you determine what your case is worth? The only way to know the true worth of a case is to be actively involved in resolving car accident cases in your area. That is why it is so important that you find a local car accident attorney who devotes a large amount of his or her practice to these types of cases.

Make no mistake. Negotiation is a game to some insurance company adjusters, and many are highly skilled and trained negotiators. The adjuster usually begins with a minimal offer to see if the injured victim will bite. In most cases, an initial offer is not fair compensation and you should not accept it.

INSIDER TIP
Negotiating a car accident settlement with an insurance company takes skill, experience, knowledge of the law, and an understanding of the value of your injuries. Only a local car accident lawyer should conduct the negotiation with an auto insurance company.

The "game" continues and your attorney demands more money from the adjuster. At this time, the adjuster usually increases the offer. Sometimes, this game goes back and forth for months at a time. Auto insurance companies are known for this tactic. They hope to wear you down so that you will give up and settle your case at an amount less than fair compensation. All the while negotiations are under way, the insurance company keeps the money in its bank accounts, making interest and income on money that should be yours.

An experienced lawyer will push an adjuster as far as possible until the insurance company makes its final offer. The insurance company will eventually make a "take it or leave it" offer. At this point, your lawyer should meet with you to evaluate your case and discuss with you the pros and cons of either taking your case to court or accepting the offer. Your lawyer should make a recommendation as to the likelihood of success and the costs and risks of going to trial. If you decide not to settle your case, the next step is to file a lawsuit.

Before filing a lawsuit, your lawyer should educate you about how personal injury cases are conducted in your jurisdiction. Jurisdiction means the county where your case will be filed. Each county in your state has its own set of procedures, judges, and most importantly, juries with differing views of car accident cases and injury victims.

INSIDER TIP

Before filing a lawsuit, you must analyze the value of your injuries, disabilities, and lost wages. You must also consider the costs of litigation and trial, especially the high cost of in-court medical testimony. Finally, you must determine your chances of winning in conjunction with the case value and the costs involved in your jurisdiction.

History has proven that some counties are more willing than others to award fair compensation for your injuries. It is important to note that many suburban counties are very conservative and may not fairly compensate a car accident victim for pain and suffering. An experienced personal injury attorney will know the general trends of jury awards in your jurisdiction and will be best prepared to evaluate any settlement offers before filing a lawsuit.

Section Ten:
What Does a Lawsuit Involve?

The first step of a lawsuit is to prepare and file a complaint with the court in the proper jurisdiction. If you are the person filing the complaint, you are known as the plaintiff. The other party, against whom you are filing the complaint, is known as the defendant.

A complaint is a legal document that states who you are and why you are suing. A complaint is very specific and should be prepared only by a lawyer. States have strict rules regarding the content of the complaint and how it should be formatted. Failure to follow these rules could result in the rejection of your complaint and dismissal of your case forever.

INSIDER TIP
Do not attempt to prepare and file
a lawsuit without the help of an
experienced car accident lawyer.

After the complaint has been filed with the court, it must be delivered to the defendant by a county sheriff. This is called "service." There are special rules regarding the proper manner and timing of service.

After being served with the complaint, the defendant has a certain time period in which to file an "answer" to the complaint. An answer is a paragraph-by-paragraph response to the plaintiff's complaint, either admitting or denying the plaintiff's allegations.

After the complaint and answer are filed, the "discovery" phase begins. At this point, both the plaintiff and defendant are required by state court rules to share certain facts, documents, and information about the case. There are several parts to the discovery phase. The first part of the discovery phase in a car accident case is where the plaintiff and defendant send each other a list of questions that each must answer under oath. These questions are called "interrogatories."

In car accident cases, interrogatories generally ask how the accident occurred, about the plaintiff's medical treatment, lost wages, pain and suffering, and about insurance coverage. A lawyer should meet with his or her client to properly prepare a truthful response to each question.

INSIDER TIP

During the litigation process, it is extremely important to keep in contact with your lawyer. Many decisions must be made that should include input from the injured client.

Unfortunately for some clients, their lawyers send the interrogatory questions directly to them by mail and never meets to discuss the questions and to prepare truthful answers that best protect their client's interests. This type of lawyering is a disservice to the client because the answers to these questions can be used to discredit the plaintiff at trial.

At the same time as the interrogatories are exchanged, lawyers often send requests for production of documents. Each side must "produce," or turn over, papers and documents relative to the case. For example, the plaintiff must turn over the police report, all medical records and reports, and most other written documents relevant to the accident and the claim. Written correspondence between the plaintiff and his or her lawyer is protected from "discovery" and, in most cases, is not provided to the opposing party.

 INSIDER TIP
During the litigation process, it is extremely important to keep in contact with your lawyer. Many decisions must be made that should include input from the injured client.

At this point, the defendant has the right to hire a "defense" doctor to examine the plaintiff and formulate an opinion about the plaintiff's condition. The defense doctor will issue a report and, if necessary, testify at trial. "Defense" doctors are hired to attack the plaintiff's claim by minimizing the plaintiff's injuries, pain, and suffering.

The defense medical examination is extremely important. An experienced car accident lawyer advises his or her client about what to expect during the defense medical examination and how to truthfully respond to questions asked by the examiner in a way that will minimize any damage to the plaintiff's case. The lawyer will also advise his or her client on which questions not to answer. A client's ill-preparedness for this type of examination can be fatal to the case.

After this initial period of sharing information, the defense attorney sends a notice for the plaintiff's deposition. This is a legal notice that requires you to appear and give testimony about the case. A deposition is an interview that sometimes turns into an interrogation. Other than trial, a deposition is the most intimidating part of the lawsuit process.

You, your attorney, the defense attorney(s), the defendant, and a court reporter are usually present at a deposition. A deposition is typically held in a law office conference room. The defense attorney is entitled to ask the plaintiff almost any question regarding the car accident, the plaintiff's medical history, treatment, and life in general.

When you file a lawsuit, you open your entire health and medical history to question. Some of the questions that a defense attorney asks are very personal, such as questions about your sexual relations, prior mental health issues, or substance abuse problems.

A dedicated lawyer will help you by going over all of the details of your medical history, treatment, and other aspects of the case in preparation for your deposition. Retain an attorney who will have the time to review the records and properly prepare you for your deposition.

About a month or two before trial is scheduled, motions are filed by the parties. A motion is a request of the court to rule on a particular legal issue that has developed in the case. There are different motions that may be filed, but the most common type in a personal injury case is a motion for summary judgment. A motion for summary judgment is commonly filed by the defense to have your case thrown out of court. This routinely occurs in limited tort (verbal threshold) cases when the defense believes that your case may not be serious enough to pass the limited tort requirements. Refer to Section Six for more information regarding limited tort auto insurance.

A plaintiff's response to a summary judgment motion must be a detailed legal response expressing why the case should not be dismissed. An experienced car accident lawyer will keep current on the constantly changing court opinions that trial judges rely upon to determine whether a case is serious enough to pass the limited tort test. Once the motions are decided, and if your case survives summary judgment, your case will be scheduled for trial.

At this point, if your case has not settled, you will need to prepare to fight the final and most difficult battle. Your strength and resolve will be tested at trial. You must be prepared both physically and mentally. You must know your case, inside and out. You must be familiar with your treatment and your prior statements, and you must be prepared to deal with whatever the defense has in store for you.

Your attorney should prepare you for direct and cross-examination. You should practice getting on the witness stand and speaking to a judge or jury. You should learn to think on your feet and learn how to deal with the "bad facts" in your case.

You must also learn to control your emotions in court, whether you are overly emotional or not emotional at all. You must be credible to a jury. Being "credible" means that the jury or judge must find you to be honest and believable when testifying. It is important to note that many injured car accident victims tell the truth on the witness stand (as they are required to) but, for whatever reason, the jury does not believe them. This may be due to personality, demeanor, clothing, nervous habits, or way of public speaking. A good trial lawyer will make you aware of and attempt to correct any impediments that you may have.

 INSIDER TIP
You must be an honest and credible person to recover in a personal injury lawsuit. You cannot fool a jury by being deceptive or exaggerating your injuries.

Just remember that no matter how much you and your attorney prepare, if your case proceeds to trial, the outcome is never certain.

Section Eleven:
What Should I Do Now?

1. First and foremost, do not talk to the other driver or his or her insurance company. Much like a criminal case, anything you say may be used against you in your claim. If you do answer a phone call from that company, politely tell the caller that you have consulted with a lawyer and that your lawyer will be contacting him or her shortly.

2. Follow up with your family doctor at your first opportunity. Set up an appointment no more two days after the car accident. If your family doctor is not comfortable treating car accident patients, ask to be referred to another doctor.

3. Preserve all physical evidence. Take pictures of your car and, if possible, the other car. Take pictures of the scene and surroundings in all directions where the car accident took place. Take pictures of any skid marks and any debris on the roadway at the time of the accident. If your injuries are visible, take pictures of your injuries daily. Safeguard these photos both physically and electronically.

4. Obtain a copy of the police accident report. The police officer who responded to the scene will prepare a crash report. It usually takes the police department a week or two to complete the report. Local or state police departments may charge you a nominal fee for the report.

5. Keep a daily journal in a sturdy notebook. In it, document all telephone calls that you make and receive regarding your case. Document your pain, prescribed and over-the-counter medications, and medical treatment. Keep a list of the names and addresses of all of your medical providers.

6. Consult with an experienced local car accident lawyer. A local lawyer should provide you with the best insight about local insurance company adjusters and juries. Most, if not all, car accident lawyers offer a free consultation.

Be aware that on the day of your car accident, you entered a war zone. Insurance companies have spent the last 30 years warping public opinion so that many people believe that injured accident victims do not deserve fair compensation. If your case is properly prepared from the beginning, you will have your best chance to recover what you deserve – fair compensation. Nothing more and nothing less!

About the Author

Michael L. Saile, Jr., Esq. has been representing injured car accident victims throughout his career. Mr. Saile graduated from the University of Delaware with a bachelor's degree in the Science of Accounting. Following college, Mr. Saile attended Widener University School of Law, where he participated in the school's trial advocacy association. After successfully passing both the Pennsylvania and New Jersey bar examinations, Mr. Saile began working in New Jersey to represent individuals seriously injured in car accidents.

In 2004, Mr. Saile joined his father and formed the law firm of Saile & Saile LLP, located in Newtown/Langhorne (lower Bucks County), Pennsylvania. Mr. Saile is a member of both the Pennsylvania and New Jersey Associations for Justice, which are groups of personal injury lawyers who work to improve our civil justice system.

Mr. Saile is the author of the PA–NJ Car Accident Lawyer Blog. He has been named multiple times to the Rising Star-Super Lawyer List published by Thompson Reuters, a designation only given to 2.5% of lawyers in Pennsylvania. This designation means that his peers and colleagues have recognized him as one of the top up-and-coming attorneys in the state. Mr. Saile has also recently been named to the "Top 40 Under 40" list by the National Trial Lawyers Association.

Mr. Saile especially enjoys working on car accident cases to help victims regain what they lost due to injury. He represents individuals in their fights against big and powerful auto insurance companies and takes great pride in knowing that through his hard work, he has the opportunity to make his clients' lives better.

In his free time, Mike enjoys spending time with his family, making homemade wine, golfing, exercising, fishing, winter sports, and traveling.

The law firm of Saile & Saile LLP represents car accident victims throughout the Commonwealth of Pennsylvania and the State of New Jersey. Although our office is located in Bucks County, Pennsylvania, we service clients in every county of Pennsylvania and New Jersey. If you cannot travel to our office, we can come to your home or make hospital appointments. Call or email us to schedule an appointment for a free car accident consultation. If your accident has occurred in another state, we can help you find an experienced and qualified lawyer.

WA